The Teachers, Schools, and Society

A Brief Introduction to Education *Reader*

David Miller Sadker

Karen R. Zittleman

Boston   Burr Ridge, IL   Dubuque, IA   Madison, WI   New York   San Francisco   St. Louis
Bangkok   Bogotá   Caracas   Kuala Lumpur   Lisbon   London   Madrid   Mexico City
Milan   Montreal   New Delhi   Santiago   Seoul   Singapore   Sydney   Taipei   Toronto

The McGraw·Hill Companies

Higher Education

THE TEACHERS, SCHOOLS, AND SOCIETY: A BRIEF INTRODUCTION TO
EDUCATION READER
Published by McGraw-Hill, a business unit of The McGraw-Hill Companies, Inc., 1221 Avenue
of the Americas, New York, NY, 10020. Copyright © 2007 by The McGraw-Hill Companies,
Inc. All rights reserved. No part of this publication may be reproduced or distributed in any form
or by any means, or stored in a database or retrieval system, without the prior written consent of
The McGraw-Hill Companies, Inc., including, but not limited to, in any network or other
electronic storage or transmission, or broadcast for distance learning.
Some ancillaries, including electronic and print components, may not be available to customers
outside the United States.

This book is printed on acid-free paper.

1 2 3 4 5 6 7 8 9 0 2CSS/2CSS 0 9 8 7 6 5

ISBN-13: 978-0-07-321622-5
ISBN-10: 0-07-321622-4

Cover credit: Gettyimages.com

The Internet addresses listed in the text were accurate at the time of publication. The inclusion of a Web site does
not indicate an endorsement by the authors or McGraw-Hill, and McGraw-Hill does not guarantee the accuracy of
the information presented at these sites.

www.mhhe.com

Brief Contents

Contents

Chapter 6: Philosophy of Education

Readings

Case Studies

Chapter 7: Financing and Governing America's Schools

Readings

Case Studies

Chapter 8: School Law and Ethics

Readings

Case Studies

Part 3: Schools and Classrooms

Chapter 9: Schools: Choices and Challenges

Readings

Case Studies

Chapter 10: Curriculum, Standards, and Testing

Readings

www.mhhe.com/
sadkerbrief1e

**Updated Daily! Visit the Online Learning Center
to access PowerWeb articles and today's education news.**

The Teachers, Schools, and Society: *Reader*

We wrote *Teachers, Schools, and Society: A Brief Introduction to Education* to introduce you to the field of education and provide you with an understanding of its foundations and issues. The typical textbook cannot fully explore different points of view, particular topics in depth, or practical applications of the ideas and skills described in the book. But if you are reading *Teachers, Schools, and Society,* you know it is anything but typical. We include this free reader inside the textbook, a book of exciting ideas and insights in the form of readings and case studies, to allow greater examination of important topics and issues. These readings and case studies are connected to the chapter content to provide greater depth of coverage of pressing topics than typically found in a text. (Who says you can't have it all!) We cleverly call this **The Teachers, Schools, and Society *Reader***.

Do not let the fact that this reader is on a CD-ROM fool you—it is a reader. The reader includes 46 readings from contemporary journals and historical sources, as well as 27 case studies that illustrate situations and raise issues that you may very well be confronted with as a teacher. We picked readings that are interesting and insightful, reflect different points of views, and will add to your perspective as a teacher. The case studies are focused on real life—practical problems facing teachers. They provide a reality test to the ideas in the text and the reader. You can explore them alone, with friends, or perhaps your instructor will have you work through some of these cases in class. And yes, they are based on real-life events. We enjoyed selecting the materials and hope that you will enjoy reading them.

Organization of the Readings and Cases

The readings and case studies are primarily organized by the chapters in *Teachers, Schools, and Society: A Brief Introduction to Education.* We have created a topic index—located at the end of this booklet and also on the CD-ROM—that references each reading and case to its major topics, allowing you to explore the materials in a variety of ways. Each reading and case includes analysis questions to help you reflect on the issues raised.

Connecting to Today's Headlines

This reader is dynamic and adds a depth that textbooks by nature often lack, but even a reader can miss new and exciting developments that occur after it is published. So we developed a CNN-like approach to the problem. (You can think of it as "ENN, the Educational News Network.") The readings and cases studies on the CD-ROM are enhanced by current news and research, updated regularly by PowerWeb. PowerWeb, accessible through the text's Online Learning Center, is an Education news resource with daily newsfeeds and current articles organized by topic.

Enjoy and grow from the opinions and ideas that emerge from the readings, and the challenges that confront everyday lives of teachers and are embedded in the case studies.

David Miller Sadker and
Karen R. Zittleman

Connecting to Today's Headlines

PowerWeb at www.mhhe.com/sadkerbrief1e

This reader contains our selection of some of the best articles we think you should read about Education. However, every day there is breaking news and research to inform your understanding of education and teaching. To connect you to current headlines and opinions, we invite you to link to PowerWeb. Through PowerWeb you will be able to access daily newsfeeds and current articles to keep you on the cutting edge of Education news and research.

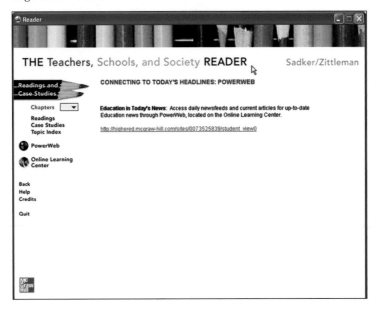

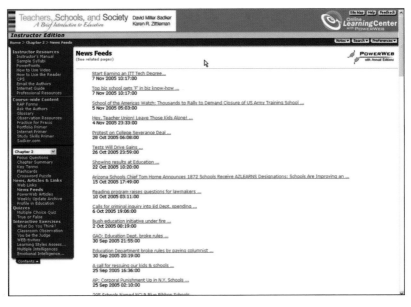

Getting Started

System Requirements

In order to run this CD-ROM properly; please make sure that your computer meets the minimum system requirements:

Minimum requirements:

For Windows:

Intel Pentium II 200, Windows 2000, XP, or NY 4.0 +; 32 MB of available memory, color monitor, Adobe Acrobat Reader

For Macintosh OSX:

G3 running 10.1 or better; 128 MB of available RAM, Adobe Acrobat Reader

For Macintosh Classic:

Power Macintosh 180 (G3 recommended) system 9.0 or later; 32 MB available RAM, color monitor, Adobe Acrobat Reader

Starting the CD-ROM

Windows

1. Insert the CD into the CD-ROM drive.

2. The CD should start automatically.

If it does not:

1. Double click on My Computer on your desktop.

2. Double click on CD-ROM drive option, most commonly called the D:/ drive.

3. Double click on the start_here.exe file from the CD-ROM.

Macintosh

1. Insert the CD into the CD-ROM drive.

2. The CD should start automatically.

If it does not:

1. Double click on the Sadker CD-ROM.

3. Double click on the start_here file from the CD-ROM.

If you need service to install this program, please call 1-800-331-5094 between 9am and 5pm EST.

The Teaching Profession and You

Chapter 1

Readings

Case Studies

Reading 1.1

Keeping Good Teachers: Why It Matters, What Leaders Can Do

Linda Darling Hammond
Educational Leadership, May 2003

Teacher retention is a function of how schools hire teachers and how schools use their resources. Teacher turnover is 50 percent higher in high-poverty schools than in low-poverty schools, and first-year teachers leave urban schools at much higher rates than do their suburban counterparts. Since teacher effectiveness increases sharply after the first few years, the costs of early teacher attrition are enormous. Early teacher attrition also subjects urban students to a continual parade of ineffective teachers. The factors influencing teacher attrition are (1) salaries, especially for younger teachers; (2) working conditions, especially as teachers gain experience (i.e., class size, teaching load, instructional materials, administrative support, teacher participation in decision making, and collegial learning opportunities); (3) teacher preparation and training, including formal teacher education and student teaching experience; and (4) state induction programs for new teachers and mentoring programs in the first years of teaching. The bottom line is that teachers will stay where they are if they feel appreciated and supported in their work.

Analysis Questions

1. Are mentoring programs for new teachers cost-effective? Explain why or why not.
2. What benefits do mentors draw from mentoring programs for new teachers?
3. Is it cost-effective for states to invest in short-term alternative certification programs for new teachers to meet teacher hiring needs? Explain why or why not.
4. The author offers four reasons for teacher attrition. Do you see any of these as more or less important? Would you add any to this list?
5. Depending on your intended grade level and subject area for your first year of teaching, describe your expectations of a mentoring program and your own personal ideal mentor.

Reading 1.2

How to Build a Better Teacher

Robert Holland
Policy Review, April/May 2001

Effective teachers are the single most important factor in student achievement, and America's schools need more effective teachers. Currently, entry into the teaching profession is controlled and regulated by a combination of state departments of education, university schools of education, teacher unions, and NCATE, the National Council for Accreditation of Teacher Education. Some educators would like to tighten regulation of teacher hiring even further through a centralized, national system of teacher licensing. The author of this article proposes to deregulate and decentralize teacher hiring. Instead of screening new teachers according to pedagogy courses completed and degrees earned, school administrators should be free to hire the most intellectually promising candidates and let the schools assimilate them in the nitty-gritty of preparing lesson plans and classroom management. Using an approach adopted in New Jersey, principals would place new teachers under the tutelage of mentors. Using the Tennessee Value-Added Assessment System, schools would regularly measure the impact of individual teachers on their students' achievement. The education establishment deems credentials and licensure to be the equivalent of teacher quality assurance. The goal of the author's suggested alternative approach is to provide new teachers with on-the-job training in applied teaching under the supervision of veteran teacher-mentors and to measure the quality and effectiveness of new (and other) teachers based on real-world academic results from the classroom.

Analysis Questions

1. As a teacher education student, how do you respond to the critics of pedagogy courses in this article?
2. Do you agree with the author's criticism of the role of teacher unions in the current system for teacher certification? Explain why or why not.
3. What do you think of the author's proposal for deregulating and decentralizing teacher hiring?
4. Do you have your own proposal for revamping the current system for teacher certification, perhaps one that marries elements of the current system with elements of the author's proposal or your own brand-new ideas?
5. What might be the potential problems if the author's approach is adopted?

Reading 1.3

Metaphors of Hope

Mimi Brodsky Chenfeld
Phi Delta Kappan, December 2004

Looking beyond the negative, pessimistic media coverage of American education today, the author has in her travels found hundreds of teachers who have, in often challenging circumstances, created positive classrooms built on mutual respect, caring, support, and cooperation. The author tells the stories of three such teachers (Tom Tenerovich, Cathy Arment, and Dee Gibson). She also describes the work of two educational consultants (Anne Price and Claudette Cole), who help school administrators, teachers, and staff understand that they need to create climates of mutual respect, caring, support, and cooperation for themselves as well as their students. Without that commitment and belief, even the best structures and strategies for creating genuine classroom communities are unlikely to succeed.

Analysis Questions

1. What is the ultimate benefit of the Town Meetings in Tom Tenerovich's classroom?
2. Would you use Town Meetings in your classroom? Why or why not? If so, in the same way or in a different way?
3. Why was it difficult for Cathy Arment to articulate the strategies or methods behind her caring and supportive classroom community?
4. What you would say in a new *Welcome to the Family* card for Dee Gibson to use next year?
5. Do you think Anne Price and Claudette Cole's consulting work with school administrators, teachers, and staff is necessary and important? Explain why or why not.

Case Study 1.1

Megan Brownlee: A parent visits her children's favorite elementary school teacher and is surprised to discover that the teacher does not encourage her to enter the teaching profession.

Analysis Question

1. Identify the problems Megan Brownlee describes to Terri Ernst.

2. How significant are these problems, do you think?

Case Study 1.2

Jennifer Gordon: A mature woman beginning a second career as an elementary school teacher struggles during her student teaching experience with how to deal with her cooperating teacher who treats her very badly and corrects her in front of the class.

Analysis Questions

1. How would you describe the problem in this case?

2. What can Jennifer do? What might she have done earlier?

Chapter 2

Diverse Learners

Readings

Case Studies

Reading 2.1

Text Excerpt from *Race Matters*

Cornel West
Beacon Press, 1993, 2001

The author of this book sees a decline in racial relations and a return to segregation in American society, and believes that the very limited public discussion of these issues is misdirected; it focuses on the "problems" of black people, instead of the flaws of American society. Liberal Americans view black "problems" as an economic issue, and conservative Americans view black "problems" as issues of morality and values. The author calls for a new framework and a new language for racial issues that are grounded in the acceptance of "the basic humanness and Americanness" of each and every one of us. Simply put, black Americans are not "them"; they are "us." We, all Americans, need to rely on ourselves and our common history, focus on the common good, and choose visionary leaders to make our ideals of freedom, democracy and equality a reality for all of us. One essential step is some form of large-scale public intervention, with the assistance of business and labor, to ensure basic social goods—housing, food, health care, and education—for all Americans, especially children. The author has hope that "the vast intelligence, imagination, humor, and courage of Americans" will carry the day.

Analysis Questions

1. Do you agree that America, on the whole, has been historically weak-willed in ensuring racial justice and has continued to resist fully accepting the humanity of blacks? Explain why or why not.

2. Do you think America has made progress, or lost ground, in this area since the author published his book in 1993?

3. Do you view Cornell West as a radical or as a pragmatist?

4. How do we go about achieving the author's vision of a "genuine multiracial democracy" where there are no "thems" and everyone is included in "We, the people"?

5. Can you identify any trends or developments in America or any new leaders that give hope to the author's vision of a "genuine multiracial democracy" in America?

Reading 2.2

Language Learning: A Worldwide Perspective

Donna Christian, Ingrid U. Pufahl, and Nancy C. Rhodes
Educational Leadership, December 2004/January 2005

Over the past several decades our country has marginalized the teaching and study of foreign languages at all levels of education. The United States, in short, is not "language-competent." It is only recently that government and academia have recognized the need to reverse this trend. For example, the American Council on the Teaching of Foreign Languages has designated 2005 as the Year of Languages in the United States. Many countries, including Canada and Australia, offer successful models for high-quality, effective foreign language instruction. Studies show that such programs share a number of attributes, including early compulsory language instruction; a well-articulated curriculum and assessment; strong leadership and commitment at the local, regional, and national levels of government and community; and core subject status for foreign language courses; to name only a few of the key factors.

Analysis Questions

1. Why has foreign language study become a low education priority in our country in recent years?
2. Do you think the United States needs to make the same commitment to foreign language study as the Council of Europe has made for the member countries of the European Union? Explain why or why not.
3. Do you think our country should follow the Canadian model and become an officially bilingual (English-Spanish) country with heritage language programs for other languages? Explain why or why not.
4. Do you think this article is much ado about nothing, or do you think that it presents a point of view that should be taken seriously?
5. If you had a choice, would you choose to have learned a foreign language at a young age? Explain.

Reading 2.3

Profoundly Multicultural Questions

Sonia M. Nieto
Educational Leadership, December 2002/January 2003

To give all students of all backgrounds an equal opportunity to learn, multicultural education must be accompanied by equal access to educational resources for all students. Unfortunately, widespread and entrenched inequities plague our public schools, especially in urban areas. At the same time that students of color are increasing in our schools, the achievement gap between white students and students of color is widening, as is the gap in school financing for urban and suburban schools. The author asks probing questions about the lack of access to high-level academic courses for urban students; continuing *de facto* racial and ethnic segregation in and between schools; low levels of training, experience, and diversity among urban teachers; and public school financing that bears no realistic relationship to the relative needs of urban and suburban students.

Analysis Questions

1. Why is it so difficult for American society at large to recognize and grapple with the gap between the reality and the promise of public education in so many of our schools?
2. How should we attack the problem of *de facto* racial and ethnic segregation in our public schools?
3. How can we attract and retain better trained and more experienced teachers in urban public schools?
4. What alternative system of public school financing would you propose to eliminate the inequities in school financing between urban and suburban areas?
5. Should your pedagogical training involve multicultural teaching methods? Why or why not?

Reading 2.4

Discipline and the Special Education Student

James A. Taylor and Richard A. Baker, Jr.
Educational Leadership, December 2001/January 2002

In 1997 Congress amended the Individuals with Disabilities Education Act (IDEA) to clarify that schools cannot allow students with learning disabilities (LD) to disrupt learning environments and that, with limited exceptions for certain long-term changes of placement for LD students, LD students are subject to schoolwide disciplinary procedures. This clarification confirms Congress' overriding intent that LD students participate as fully as possible in mainstream school curriculum and life. The author explains that comprehensive disciplinary procedures for students with or without disabilities should focus on preventive discipline and supportive discipline before corrective discipline. When preventive or supportive approaches sometimes fail, fair and effective corrective discipline is based on well-known guidelines for natural consequences for disciplinary infractions that disrupt the learning environment.

Analysis Questions

1. Why did Congress amend the IDEA in 1997 to clarify that, with limited exceptions, LD students must be disciplined in the same manner as students without disabilities?
2. Why should teachers first take preventive and supportive approaches to classroom discipline issues before resorting to corrective discipline? Give an example of each.
3. Should students have input and participate in the formulation of classroom procedures and rules? Explain why or why not.
4. Explain the following statement in terms of LD students: "All students deserve well-disciplined learning environments that are fun, focused, and full of creative energy"?
5. Would you react the same way if a student with disabilities misbehaved as opposed to a student without disabilities? Explain.

Case Study 2. 1

Carol Brown: A teacher, after socially integrating a diverse class, sees her efforts threatened when a child's pencil case disappears and is thought to have been stolen. Her students' reactions are not what she had expected.

Analysis Questions

1. What is Carol Brown's problem?
2. What do you think are Carol's objectives for her class?

3. What should Carol have done?
4. What should she do now?

Case Study 2.2

Carolyn Davis: An experienced first grade teacher who has been an inclusion teacher for three years expresses her frustration with the inclusion process.

Analysis Questions

1. Based on the information in this case, what are the pros and cons of inclusive classrooms?
2. Do you support inclusive classrooms? Why or why not?

3. Would you teach in an inclusive classroom? Why or why not?

Case Study 2.3

Joan Martin, Marilyn Coe, and Warren Groves: A classroom teacher, a special education teacher, and a principal hold different views about mainstreaming a boy with poor reading skills. The dilemma comes to a head over the method of grading him at the end of the marking period.

Analysis Questions

1. What should be done about Donald?
2. What advice would you give Joan as to the position she should take in the meeting? Marilyn? Warren?
3. From your other reading, what suggestions would you make to Joan about what she might do in her class to enhance the possibilities of success for Donald? What else might Marilyn do?

Chapter 3

Student Life in School and at Home

Readings

Case Studies

Reading 3.1

Bullying Among Children

Janis R. Bullock
Childhood Education, Spring 2002

In spite of the popular notion that bullying is just a normal part of growing up, research shows that such behavior can lead to many problems, including violent outbursts, increased school absenteeism, and dangerous acts of retaliation. Bullying requires intervention, and this article describes intervention plans at the school, classroom, and individual levels. These intervention plans include parent involvement, peer mediation, and direct discussions about bullying in classroom.

Analysis Questions

1. Why and how has bullying been allowed to flourish in the American school system?

2. How can teachers, parents, and administrators identify the characteristics of bullies and victims?

3. Describe how Janis R. Bullock suggests that teachers handle bullying cases in their classrooms.

4. In addition to the models presented in the text, what other ways might you suggest to stop bullying in schools?

Reading 3.2

Differentiating Sexualities in Singular Classrooms

Kevin J. Graziano
Multicultural Education, Winter 2003

As members of a minority group despised by some people in our society, gay and lesbian students face social isolation, rejection by family, depression, low self-esteem, suicide risk, harassment, and acts of violence. The American educational system is essentially blindfolded and mute on the subject of homosexuality, and educators feel unprepared and reluctant to deal with gay and lesbian issues. The author recounts the harrowing story of his own life of painful isolation and grim survival as a young gay teenager. By his senior year in high school, he had evolved from a mere survivor of school to a successful academic and extracurricular student, successes pursued as a refuge from his sexuality. The author desires that schools become safe havens for all students, including gay and lesbian students. He hopes that gay and lesbian students will be free from harassment and victimization and will see themselves in the curriculum, texts, and hallways as a respected part of the school community.

Analysis Questions

1. As a teacher, would you take the author up on his suggestion that you attend a gay student association event, attend sensitivity training, or include the topic of homosexuality in a course where relevant? Explain why or why not.

2. From your experience as a student, do you agree with the author's description of our educational system and educators regarding the treatment of the subject of homosexuality? Explain why or why not.

3. As a teacher, do you think the diversity simulation game at the end of the article would help your students understand behaviors of belonging to majority and minority groups? Explain why or why not.

4. Do you agree with the author that educational practices are not effective without social justice and therefore that all schools must include gay and lesbian issues within the scope of multicultural education? Explain why or why not.

5. How would you combat the negative usage of the word *gay* in your classroom/school?

Reading 3.3

Meeting the Challenge of the Urban High School

Joyce Baldwin
Carnegie Reporter, Spring 2001

One source of urban educational challenges is the disconnection students feel. Too little time is spent in talk at the family dinner table, and too many children are growing up in front of the Internet or the cable television. This disconnect is mirrored in schools, where many students search unsuccessfully for adults who can guide and mentor them. But there are urban schools such as Bel Air High School and Urban Academy that have succeeded by creating smaller schools where students feel less anonymous, more connected, and educationally challenged. Other factors in student and urban school success, Baldwin explains, are parent involvement and programs that smooth the transition from middle school to high school.

Analysis Questions

1. What are some ways that schools may get more crucial involvement from parents in their child's school and academic performance?
2. What may be some of the difficulties in turning schools around such in the cases of Bel Air High and Urban Academy?
3. What are the negative and positive effects of what Baldwin calls the "shopping mall" approach to secondary education? How did it become so prevalent?
4. How has the history of education shaped today's problems/solutions at the secondary level?
5. What are some other ways that we may "re-connect" students and improve their success in school?

Reading 3.4

Creating School Climates That Prevent School Violence

Reece L. Peterson and Russell Skiba
The Clearing House, January/February 2001

School climate is defined as "the feelings that students and staff have about the school environment over a period of time." Video cameras and metal detectors, devices that are in place to ensure safety, can create a negative school climate. However, Peterson and Skiba suggest several ways to improve the school climate. Parent involvement, for example, is important for increasing attendance rates and lowering suspension rates. On the other hand, well-implemented bullying prevention and peer mediation programs have shown promise in improving school climate. Character education, on the other hand, is widely used to improve school climate despite the lack of empirical evidence of its effectiveness. A positive school climate is central to preventing school violence and improving the quality of academic life in school.

Analysis Questions

1. What are the challenges and obstacles in attracting parents to programs such as PASS and PATCH?
2. How can Character Counts and other such programs be added to schools without detracting from time set aside for the academic topics?
3. How can peer mediation be successfully implemented?
4. What issues negatively affect school climate—and how can a positive school climate be promoted?

Reading 3.5

Profiles in Caring: Teachers Who Create Learning Communities in Their Classrooms

David Strahan, Tracy W. Smith, Mike McElrath,
and Cecilia M. Toole
Middle School Journal, September 2001

Learning communities have a shared sense of purpose, norms of collegiality, rituals that celebrate achievement, and heroes and heroines, and they are places where joy and humor abound. This article describes three distinctly different classrooms. Despite the teachers' different approaches, successful learning communities were evident in each case. Betty placed students in groups where they were allowed to socialize and learn cooperatively. Jay allowed his students controlled freedom to complete their individual tasks. Darlene and Ashley played off of each other, allowing students to reap benefits and rewards for their accomplishments while involving the entire community. Each of these environments put the students first and emphasized the "we," merged the academic and the social, involved students in class decisions, and opened the classroom to the community.

Analysis Questions

1. What are the advantages and potential problems of involving students in decision making?
2. How does Jay prevent problems from getting out of hand when students are given greater freedom?
3. Suggest some traditions and rituals that you could implement in your classroom to recognize and celebrate student accomplishments.
4. What elements of Betty's class environment could you apply to teaching a different subject?
5. Suggest ways to involve the community in your own teaching.

Case Study 3.1

Bonnie Bradley: We spend two successive periods watching a first-year science teacher as she presents a lab to her students and then observes the students as they engage in the lab itself.

Analysis Questions

1. Given what you know about models of teaching, how would you describe Bonnie's teaching?
2. What is her management style?
3. Are her students learning good science?

Case Study 3.2

Richard Carlton: We follow a second-grade teacher during his morning routine, which focuses on literacy instruction. The teacher has three included children in the classroom.

Analysis Questions

1. Pretend you just observed Richard's class. Write down your observations.
2. What did you think that Richard did especially well? What aspects of Richard's teaching or classroom did not make sense to you?

Case Study 3.3

Anne Holt: This case follows an experienced teacher through her morning routine with a diverse group of first grade children. The case presents a detailed look at her organization and the climate she creates in the classroom.

Analysis Questions

1. Pretend you just observed Anne's class. Write down your observations.
2. What did you think that Anne did especially well? What aspects of Anne's teaching or classroom did not make sense to you?

The History of American Education

Readings

Reading 4.1

Text Excerpt from *The Education of Free Men*

Horace Mann
From *Tenth Annual Report* and *Twelfth Annual Report*, 1846
and 1848

Not educating youth is comparable to infanticide! With this powerful declaration Horace Mann zealously argues for the education of all citizens and the great potential that lies within every child. He argues that the right to education is a divine right and that not to educate all youth is like killing their souls. Children are the "raw material" ready to be educated, religiously and otherwise, in order fit into the fraternity of America. Mann contends that if a child is trained right, he/she will grow up to be morally exceptional and an asset to society. Education, he says, is the great equalizer. For all of these reasons and more, Mann demands free education for all citizens.

Analysis Questions

1. What are some of the strong points of Mann's argument? What elements of debate does he employ here?
2. Which phrases and arguments would not work today as a demand for free, public schools? How would you update this petition for today's times?
3. What are some of the flaws of Mann's argument? What may have been arguments against his work then?
4. How is education the "great equalizer of the conditions of men"?
5. How does Mann both connect religion to education and yet separate it from education?

Reading 4.2

The Changing Landscape of U.S. Education

James C. Carper
Kappa Delta Pi Record, Spring 2001

America appears to be headed back in time, towards the Colonial era when there were many schooling options. In the Colonial period, the line between private and public schools was blurred. All kinds of schools flourished, as did home schooling. The labels *private* and *public* were not clearly defined, and most schools, religious and public, received funding from both private and public sources. Religiously affiliated schools were doing a "public" service and were often funded by public money. On the other hand, many public schools demanded application fees and tuition in addition to land taxations. The major defining split between public and private schools did not emerge until the mid-19th century. Horace Mann's common school movement ushered in a new, more uniform definition of public schools that eventually led to many decades of uniform public education. Carper's article traces this history and shows how today's semipublic charter and magnet schools, along with the rise of home schooling and Protestant schools, are again blurring the public/private line and adding more diverse institutional options for students.

Analysis Questions

1. How might the new rise in the diversity of schooling options positively affect education in America? How might it negatively influence education?

2. Does there need to be a distinction between public and private schools in terms of pedagogical approach? Funding? Testing?

3. How do you interpret the current increase in home schooling?

4. Explain how the American educational system changed for the better over the nation's history. What historical trends do you find troublesome?

5. What are your predictions for the future of public, private, and home schooling?

Reading 4.3

Dichotomizing Education: Why No One Wins and America Loses

Carl D. Glickman
Phi Delta Kappan, October 2001

"The idea is not to prove that one way is the only way but instead to allow for different conceptions of education to flourish in the marketplace of public education." According to Carl D. Glickman, schools need multiple theories and approaches to function well, and educators must be careful not to ignore or dismiss unpopular or contrary ideas. In this article, Glickman describes a sampling of differing ideas and philosophies involving education and concludes by calling for the integration of conflicting "truths" in order to best serve American schools.

Analysis Questions

1. How might one combine E. D. Hirsch, Jr.'s concept of cultural literacy with Alfie Kohn's distrust of traditional education?

2. What are the dangers of a school or classroom practicing a "single truth" or single educational philosophy?

3. Using your own criteria but drawing upon ideas of Mann, Du Bois, and various philosophies studied, describe the purpose of education in America.

4. Offer different definitions of a "well-educated person."

5. Can you identify some contradictory philosophies not included in the article? How may these differing philosophies be combined or made to coexist?

Reading 4.4

Text Excerpts from *Eighty Years and More (1815–1897): Reminiscences of Elizabeth Cady Stanton*

Elizabeth Cady Stanton

In Elizabeth Cady Stanton's world, girls were clearly the second sex. The author, despite her intellectual gifts, was not given the encouragement or resources of her male contemporaries. Through the narrator's eyes, we learn of the gender differences in treatment and educational opportunities between the sexes. The author contends that the mixing of the sexes provides a "healthy condition" and objects to separating of boys and girls. The author's life was dedicated not simply to study, but to proving her equality to men.

Analysis Questions

1. Explain the differences between what was expected of boys and what was expected of girls in this work. How has that changed? How has it not?
2. Why is it so difficult for the narrator's father to accept her as equal to her brother?
3. What seems to be the narrator's biggest motivation for studying?
4. What appears to be the relationship/conflict between religion and education?
5. Many proponents believe that single-sex schooling is more effective than coeducation. The author did not. What are your views on this issue?

Chapter 5

The Struggle for Educational Opportunity

Reading

Case Studies

Reading 5.1

The Threat of Stereotype

Joshua Aronson
Educational Leadership, November 2004

Stereotyping is far more than a political correctness issue; it can have a horrific impact on academic performance. The author describes how children at very young ages are already aware of stereotypes, and how such stereotypes can affect test performance. Aronson points to research that shows that Black students' test scores doubled when they were told that the test was not a measure of their ability, only to plunge when they were asked to indicate their race prior to the testing. Similar findings were noted with women taking math tests and Latinos taking verbal tests. Such results reflect the high level of anxiety produced by stereotypes, and the author suggests strategies to neutralize this impact, including cooperative learning.

Analysis Questions

1. Name other groups and examples (besides Blacks, women, and Latinos) that may face stereotyping that affects their performance in specific situations.

2. What are some ways that stereotyping can be curtailed in the classroom?

3. How might No Child Left Behind add to stereotyping-based performance failure? How might this be changed or amended?

4. What are some specific ways to intervene, minimize, or eliminate these problems at the elementary or secondary level?

Reading 5.2

Text Excerpts from *Narrative of the Life of Frederick Douglass: An American Slave*

Frederick Douglass
1845

It may be impossible to fully understand racism today without understanding its roots in slavery. In this excerpt from the diary of Frederick Douglass, the reader glimpses firsthand what this nation was like when teaching an African American to read or write was an act punishable by death. Fredrick Douglass was self-taught, owning his mind even as his body was sold repeatedly in slave markets. He went on to become a famous orator and writer, and eventually U.S. minister to Haiti. In this narrative, Douglass describes his determination to learn how to read and write despite the risks he encountered.

Analysis Questions

1. Why was the notion of African Americans learning to read and write such a threat to slave holders?
2. How did the institution of slavery injure slave holders?
3. Identify the techniques used by Douglass to learn how to read and write. Are they still used today?
4. In what ways does the history of slavery cast a shadow on today's schools?
5. Describe the role gender played in educating African Americans. Why were white women natural teachers, and how was this "home school" closed?

Reading 5.3

An Educator's Primer to the Gender War

David Sadker

Phi Delta Kappan, November 2002

Who rules schools, boys or girls? In this article, David Sadker illustrates that efforts to give girls more of a voice and greater opportunities in school have not deprived boys of their rights, despite the pronouncements of far right-wing ideologues who argue that girls now "rule" in school. In a facetious satire, Sadker imagines what a school would be like if girls actually did rule. The author then argues that although boys often do not fit comfortably into school culture, this fact is not the fault of girls or the feminist movement; the problem lies, rather, in the way schools themselves are operated and de-signed. To conclude that girls are in some way responsible for the problems of boys is to ignore the historical evidence to the contrary and to set up a divi-sive "gender war" where no one wins. Some salient statistics are also pre-sented to show how gender role stereotypes harm both girls and boys.

Analysis Questions

1. In what ways are schools arranged to benefit boys? To benefit girls?
2. What steps might a school district take in order to more fairly account for the needs and learning styles of its female students?
3. In light of gender biases, do you think single sex schools are a good idea? Why or why not?
4. How can students themselves help in the effort to minimize gender bias in their schools?
5. How do you explain why girls consistently achieve better classroom grades but poorer standardized test scores?

Case Study 5.1

Helen Franklin: A teacher who uses parents as volunteers to help with her unique classroom organization notices that a parent volunteer who has questioned the teacher's methods will work only with white students.

Analysis Questions

1. What problems does Helen feel she has as she walks toward her classroom this morning?
2. What are her problems from your perspective?

3. Think about Helen's relationships with parents. Are they appropriate? How should teachers and parents relate and interact?

Case Study 5.2

Leigh Scott: A teacher gives a higher-than-earned grade to a mainstreamed student on the basis of the boy's effort and attitude and is confronted by a black student with identical test scores who received a lower grade and who accuses her of racism.

Analysis Questions

1. Should Leigh be prepared to change Aaron's grade?
2. How objective should a grading system be? Do students deserve special consideration for effort?

3. How should Leigh prepare to handle the meeting with Aaron?

Case Study 5.3

Mark Siegal: A teacher is irritated by a black parent who visits him regularly, demanding better instruction for her son. The teacher believes that he has tried everything he can and that the problems rest with the child and the demanding mother.

Analysis Questions

1. What problem does Mark Siegel face? What does he think is causing the problem?
2. What might be some other problems in Mark's class?

3. What are Karim's attitudes about school?
4. What should Mark do?

Philosophy of Education

Readings

Case Studies

Reading 6.1

Text Excerpts from *Experience and Education*

John Dewey
1938

When we reject one system of education, must we reject it in its entirety? John Dewey decidedly answers "no" to this question and argues that we must not conceive of progressive education as an extreme opposite to traditional education. Progressive education was created in response to criticisms of traditional education. For Dewey, traditional education was forcing static and already-interpreted information about the past into the passive minds of young subjects who consequently were neither aware of their changing world nor able to prepare for the future. Dewey argues that students must play an integral role in their education and that there is a necessary relation between actual experience and education. He carefully articulates that not all experiences are equally educative, and that the teacher must arrange for present experiences that can be fruitfully connected with future experiences. Dewey concludes that progressive education is not a haphazard exercise in improvisation that ignores the knowledge of the past, but a designed method of education that teaches students to become acquainted with the past in order that they may appreciate the living present.

Analysis Questions

1. What does the author mean by *meaningful experiences*? Does progressive education leave room for a multiplicity of meanings?
2. Do you agree with the author that progressive education provides better and more meaningful experiences for its students than traditional education?
3. Give some examples of progressive education that you have witnessed, either as a student yourself or observing a classroom.
4. What sorts of meaningful experiences might you bring to your students as a teacher?
5. Using the progressive model, how might you teach a subject that might not readily lend itself to experimentation, such as History or English?

Reading 6.2

Pathways to Reform: Start with Values

David J. Ferrero, Jr.
Education Leadership, February 2005

How is it that schools can have similar goals and common aims, but such diverse pathways and methods of instruction? David J. Ferrero argues that in order to better understand the differences in our schools, we must revisit the normative groundwork that underpins our individual philosophy of education. We cannot empirically settle the debate about what makes a school "good" because the normative lens through which we read information inevitably colors our interpretation of empirical evidence. What should have been obvious all along, Ferrero claims, is that there are different criteria by which a school might be considered good. By acknowledging differences in our philosophies of education, we can both come to understand that there are irreducible value judgments regarding teaching methodology and recognize that this does not necessitate that good schools retain nothing in common.

Analysis Questions

1. Do you agree that different methods of schooling can both adhere to their individualistic goals and also conform to certain nationwide standards?
2. The author lists a number of questions to help in discerning one's philosophy of education. Can you think of any others?
3. Are there ways for public schools to incorporate varying philosophies of education? Give some examples of how public schools might accomplish this.
4. The author stresses that, practically speaking, pluralism with regard to values will lead to inevitable differences in philosophies of education. But suppose everyone had the same values. Should schools then be held to teaching only one curriculum by means of one method?
5. The author stresses that school choice is an important response to difference. How might we handle those students from poorer communities that will not have the money necessary to allow them to choose their preferred schools? Should local or state schools boards aid in this effort?

Reading 6.3

Teaching Themes of Care

Nel Noddings
Phi Delta Kappan, May 1995

What issues and questions lie at the core of human existence? One educator, Nel Noddings, argues that the issue of "care"—for self, other, stranger—is one such issue and that schools ought to incorporate themes of care into their curricula. High scores on standardized tests, she argues, will help students little if they do not feel cared for and learn to care for others. The use of care can help us connect the lessons we learn in various standard subjects and better achieve an understanding of the relational nature of our world. Teachers can aid in the effort to bring care into the classroom by teaching in teams, by agreeing on a theme and the central focus of care in their classrooms, and by connecting different lessons taught throughout the school year with themes of care. Care is not something that ought to be relegated to specialists; rather, care ought to be everyone's responsibility. Noddings concludes by arguing that a liberal education that neglects the question of what it is to be fully human does not warrant the name *liberal*.

Analysis Questions

1. Do you agree with the author that incorporating themes of care into schools is both an achievable and desirable goal?
2. The author gives several examples of how themes of care might manifest themselves in the curriculum. Can you think of any others?
3. Can you think of any other themes that a school might incorporate into its curriculum?
4. Theodore Sizer advocates smaller learning groups in order for students to feel continuity in their education. What other student-centered structural changes might foster a feeling of continuity and connectedness in the student's education?
5. In this era of standardized testing, do you believe there is room for themes of caring in the curriculum?

Reading 6.4

A Tale of Two Schools

Larry Cuban
Education Week, January 1998

What are the criteria by which we come to call a school "good"? In this article, Larry Cuban shows how traditionalists and progressives engaged in a debate over this very question for much of the 20th century. Cuban argues that the debate, although concerned with methods of education, is at its core really about the role that schools ought to play in society. The war of words between both sides actually amounts to an argument over the values a school should teach and the goals it ought to pursue. Whereas we tend to concentrate on the differences, Cuban argues that the allegedly different goals of both sides are not inconsistent but actually derive from the common belief that schools should pass on to the next generation certain democratic attitudes and beliefs. Cuban concludes that while one cannot prove that one method is better than another, both sorts of schools are "good" if they both achieve the individual goals they set for themselves and teach their students to think and act democratically.

Analysis Questions

1. Do you think that Cuban's criteria for judging schools might ever conflict? For instance, what if a school's individual goals conflict with the instilling of democratic values?

2. The author gives several examples of what he considers democratic values. Can you think of any others to add to this list?

3. Are you convinced that both methodologies, traditionalism and progressivism, can equally advocate democratic values?

4. Will a difference in methodology amount to an intractable difference regarding the interpretation of democratic values? Give some examples.

5. Can the other philosophies of education that we have studied teach democratic values as well?

Case Study 6.1

Brenda Forester: A preservice education student is concerned that one of her methods classes will not prepare her for teaching. Her philosophy of education is challenged when she observes a writing process classroom.

Analysis Questions

1. What is Brenda Forester's problem? Why is she reacting so negatively to Professor Garrison's approach?
2. What does Professor Garrison's approach assume about the way people learn?

3. What is the relationship between Brenda's earlier school experiences and her teaching philosophy?

Case Study 6.2

Michael Watson: A teacher finds that the assistant principal's evaluation of his class calls into question his teaching style as well as his philosophy of education. The evaluation suggests that his style and rapport with the students are getting in the way of his being more demanding.

Analysis Questions:

1. Who do you think is right, Michael or Alan? Why?

2. What do you see as Michael's strengths as a teacher? His weaknesses?

Financing and Governing America's Schools

Chapter 7

Readings

Case Studies

Reading 7.1

Text Excerpt from *Amazing Grace*

Jonathan Kozol
1991

The South Bronx, Harlem, and Washington Heights comprise the poorest congressional district in America, right next to one of the richest congressional districts, and have the largest racially segregated concentration of poor people in our nation. The author paints a very bleak picture of life, and death, for these people, especially for the children, many of whose drug-addicted parents have died from AIDS and many of whom are themselves infected with the AIDS virus. The City of New York, in fact, has a policy of channeling its sickest and most troubled families into housing in this vast ghetto. Their life in this ghetto is cold in the winter, hot in the summer, infested with roaches and rats, and surrounded by rampant drug use, homicide, and crime. Yet some of them find the spirit and energy to attend church and sings hymns of hope. Unfortunately, the author does not share this hope and asks profound and troubling questions, some of which are set out below.

Analysis Questions

1. Why does the wealthiest nation in the world treat its poorest this way? Do these children believe that they are being shunned or being hidden from society? How do you see their role here, and their role on a more spiritual plane?

2. How do certain people hold up under their terrible ordeals? How do children living in this medieval landscape face the losses that they must expect?

3. How can some human beings devalue other peoples' lives? How can the shunning of the vulnerable in time come to be perceived as natural behavior? What do we do to those who frighten us? Do we put them off, as far away as possible, and hope (as one child told the author) that they will either die or disappear?

4. Will our "powers that be" look into their hearts one day and feel the grace of God and be transformed? Will they become ashamed of what they have done or what they have accepted?

5. How do you deal with such poverty, disease, and indifference?

Reading 7.2

The Culture Builder

Roland S. Barth
Educational Leadership, May 2002

Roland Barth has a novel idea: let's create schools where the culture promotes learning. If you think this is simply a description of what schools already do, the author suggests you take a look around your school and consider the many factors that discourage learning. What does it mean when a teacher hears from a fellow colleague, "That's the way we do things around here"? The author argues that these sorts of statements reflect a school's culture, which he defines as the complex pattern of norms, attitudes, beliefs, behaviors, values, ceremonies, traditions, and myths that are deeply ingrained in the core of a school's organization. School cultures are typically resistant to change, which makes their improvement very difficult to enact. A healthy school, Barth concludes, will create an environment hospitable to human learning and make it likely that students will become lifelong learners. Achieving this kind of school is the goal of the true instructional leader.

Analysis Questions

1. Think back to your days in high school (if you can remember that far!). What would you say were some of the characteristics that defined your high school's culture?

2. What sorts of impediments stand in the way of school reform? Consider examples on local, state, and national levels.

3. The author recounts a study that identified twelve healthy cultural norms. Can you think of any others to add to this list?

4. What sorts of issues do you think are likely to be deemed "nondiscussables"? How can a teacher go about breaking through the barriers surrounding these sorts of issues?

5. How will you as a teacher counteract a culture that says to students, "Learn or we will hurt you"?

Reading 7.3

The Invisible Role of the Central Office

Kathleen F. Grove
Educational Leadership, May 2002

For all you new teachers feeling a little overwhelmed by the immense work-load you are about to take on, Kathleen Grove is here to tell you that you've got a friend—the central office. Although you might think that administrators at your district's head office do little other than push papers around their desks, the author of this article describes the demanding work assumed by the central office in one Virginia school system. From the time new teachers arrive and require orientation to the time they apply for National Board certification, the central office is there to provide an "invisible" support structure that often goes unrecognized and unappreciated. Among other things, the central office is in charge of ordering district-wide priorities, fostering leadership, training and orienting new teachers, and designing a consistent, structured curriculum. Grove argues that the central office's invisibility is precisely what makes it so efficient at providing the support and consistency necessary for a high-quality instructional program.

Analysis Questions

1. Based on all the evidence presented, what background do you think officials at the central office should have?
2. Why, do you believe, despite the strong case Grove makes, is the central office often the target of teacher criticism?
3. Do you have any ideas for improving the communication and relations between the central office and teachers?
4. Consider what would happen if you taught in this district. Would you be pleased that so many decisions would be made for you? What would you do with the extra time you gain from not being involved in certain decisions?

Case Study 7.1

David Burton: A teacher whose principal allows no challenge to his authority discovers that two students who are thought to be guilty of crashing a system-wide computer program are being given unequal punishments by the principal.

Analysis Questions

1. What should David Burton do?

2. What is the ethical principle at stake here?

Case Study 7.2

Kate Sullivan: A principal faces the problems endemic to the students served by her school, which is located in a very low socioeconomic area. Issues of drugs, poverty, neglect, hunger, and homelessness are compounded by the underfunding for the school.

Analysis Questions

1. What are the issues at North Hills Elementary from Kate Sullivan's perspective?
2. What are the problems at this school from your perspective?

3. What should Kate do to improve the test scores and attendance at North Hills?
4. What should she do about Miguel?

Case Study 7.3

Jane Vincent: A teacher is asked by her principal to reconsider her grading of a student whose numerical average for the marking period is just below the department's cutoff score for that grade.

Analysis Questions

1. What dilemma is Jane facing with Willie?
2. Why, do you think, did the math department agree to the current grading system? What are the implications for Jane if she compromises it?
3. What should Jane do?

Chapter 8

School Law and Ethics

Readings

Case Studies

Reading 8.1

How Not to Teach Values: A Critical Look at Character Education

Alfie Kohn
Phi Delta Kappan, February 1998

Does the recent trend in teaching "values" equate to teaching children the righteousness of merely "behaving"? The author suggests that this may, unfortunately, be the case. He goes on to suggest that we look very carefully at the many programs designed to teach character education and to consider other possibilities for reaching the desired goal of helping children become thoughtful and decent human beings. Many of the current character educator programs teach children obedience and "good" behavior: stand straight, be quiet, do what you are told when you are told, and do not question the rules or values that are being taught. Moreover, he suggests that by rewarding children for altruistic behavior we are actually decreasing their motivation to continue such behavior. A closer look at the actual cause of what appears to be valueless behavior would be a good start. Kohn advocates a realistic look at what and how we teach values as we consider developing values programs.

Analysis Questions

1. The author suggests that "children who receive positive reinforcement for caring, sharing, and helping—are less likely than other children to keep doing those things." Can you offer a personal example of this?

2. Make two lists. First, using this article or your own school experience, list traits that are taught as "character education." Second, create your own list of traits that you would teach as character education. Compare the two. Is there a gap? How do you interpret the results of this activity?

3. Is "bad" behavior a function of being bad or a function of environmental influences? The author suggests political and economic realities may be the cause and not some inherent "badness." Do you agree or disagree? Explain.

4. Some would suggest that we teach values just by existing—that our behavior role models values that children are learning. What is the implication of this statement?

5. Some character educators will argue that it is not necessary to "reinvent the wheel." What does this mean? Do you agree? Explain.

Reading 8.2

Teaching About Religion

Susan Black
American School Board Journal, April 2003

Most educators and scholars are in agreement that the teaching of religion does indeed have a place in our schools. The author provides a useful summary to assist educators in understanding the guidelines and limitations that must be considered when teaching religion. It is a matter of educating students about religion while upholding constitutional rights. Key elements to consider in the teaching of religion are teaching without bias and keeping personal beliefs private, and knowing which topics are allowable in the study of religion. In addition, under certain conditions, students must be allowed to express their own beliefs about religion without experiencing negative consequences or discrimination. The lack of teacher training and a low teacher's comfort level in this area are additional issues that need to be addressed.

Analysis Questions

1. What are the benefits of teaching about religions in school?
2. List three or four factors for educators to remember when teaching religion.
3. Offer several examples of "unconstitutional instruction" of religion. Have you had any personal experiences of appropriate or inappropriate religious instruction? If so, briefly describe them.
4. How does your teaching institution rank in the teaching of religion? Be specific in terms of subject offerings and grade levels. Do you believe it is adequate? Do teachers receive adequate training?
5. Briefly describe the legally allowable issues in the teaching of religion as defined in the "Federal Guidelines for Religious Expression in Public Schools."

Reading 8.3

Decisions That Have Shaped U.S. Education

Perry Zirkel
Educational Leadership, December 2001/January 2002

Court decisions determine much of what we can and cannot do in the class-room today. This article provides a thumbnail sketch of the "landmark" cases regarding education. They range in topics from the famous *Brown* v. *Board of Education of Topeka* school desegregation case to issues such as equality in education, freedom of expression, student discipline, and safety and the role of religion. More recent cases involve such controversial topics as prayer in school, sexual harassment, drug testing, and student searches.

Analysis Questions

1. In the *San Antonio Independent School District* v. *Rodriguez* case, the court's decision held that the Fourteenth Amendment's equal protection clause permits any kind of financing system and requires only that a "minimum" education be provided every student: not "equal" but "minimum." Do you agree with this decision? Explain.

2. The *New Jersey* v. *T.L.O.* (1985) Supreme Court case ruled in favor of school authorities for student searches. Do you agree with this ruling? Why or why not?

3. Which of the Supreme Court rulings in this article will affect you the most as a teacher? Explain.

4. Select one of the rulings in this article and argue against the position the court took.

5. Whether the majority of the members of the Supreme Court are "liberal" or "conservative" has an enormous impact on the court's decisions. How is your life as a teacher affected by the politics of the court? (Feel free to use the cases described in this article in formulating your response.)

Reading 8.4

Andy's Right to Privacy in Grading and the *Falvo* v. *Owasso Public Schools* Case

Stephen J. Friedman
Clearing House, November/December 2002

Would you, as a teacher, require students to grade one another's papers and then ask that the grade be called out publicly in the class for recording purposes? Have you been a student in a class where that was done? Is this a violation of a student's rights to privacy? Friedman follows the progression of this case all the way to the Supreme Court. After the Owasso Public School system refused Mrs. Falvo's request to stop the peer grading practice, she began the court battle to protect her children from what she viewed as a humiliating classroom practice. During the proceedings, the Falvos' attorney argued that rights already established by FERPA and the Fourteenth Amendment were being violated. Lawyers for the opposition, the Owasso Public School system, argued that the record (or grade) is not protected until it is actually in the grade book. Although the courts differed in their decisions, the Supreme Court, in the end, voted in favor (9–0) of Owasso Public Schools.

Analysis Questions

1. What are the disadvantages of peer grading and public announcing of grades in a classroom?
2. What are the advantages of peer grading and public announcing of grades in a classroom?
3. Do you agree with the decision handed down by the Circuit Court justices or by the Supreme Court justices? Explain your position.
4. What is the impact on students when placed in a potentially embarrassing or humiliating situation? Are there ethical issues to consider?
5. Have you witnessed or experienced similar school practices where the privacy of students is put at risk? Explain.

Case Study 8.1

Amanda Jackson: A teacher discovers that her principal has a drinking problem, which is well known but never discussed among the staff. She faces a dilemma when she realizes that the principal is planning to drive a student home during a snowstorm.

Analysis Questions

1. What is going on here? What are Amanda Jackson's problems?

2. What should she do? What are the implications of the actions you suggest?

Case Study 8.2

Ellen Norton: A teacher whose concern for a shy, underachieving student has led to the student becoming her "shadow," learns that another student may be the victim of child abuse at home. The teacher has to decide if she should become involved.

Analysis Questions

1. What are Ellen Norton's problems?

2. How did Ellen get herself into this predicament?

Case Study 8.3

Diane News: In a school district beginning a gifted and talented program, a teacher must choose four students to recommend for the program from her class, but she has five potential candidates. The parent of one of the students has threatened her if she does not recommend his daughter.

Analysis Questions

1. Diane News must make a tough choice. List and compare the district's selection criteria for the G & T program to Diane's.

2. Who should she pick? Why?

Chapter 9

Schools: Choices and Challenges

Readings

Case Studies

Reading 9.1

Questionable Assumptions About Schooling

Elliot W. Eisner
Phi Delta Kappan, May 2003

We all seem to appreciate that our nation's schools are not only responsible for educating our children, but ultimately play a central role in our nation's development and direction. The author points out that because of school's great importance, we should take the time to examine some of the basic practices of public education. Unfortunately, we rarely do. In this article, Eisner describes 12 "questionable assumptions" about our public school system. For example, does organizing our students into groups of 30 to be taught by one teacher for one year, at the end of which everyone is "reshuffled," make the most sense? Many of these assumptions are so basic to schooling that we may have not ever thought to question them. But that is our shortcoming. Reform of any kind can only occur if we begin to question and discuss what we are currently doing.

Analysis Questions

1. Eisner suggests that schools abandon the idea of getting all students to the same place at the same time and instead look to "increase the variance in student performance, while escalating the mean." Do you agree or disagree? Give one example of how a school could accomplish this.

2. What are the advantages of teachers staying with a group of children through several years of education? What are the disadvantages? As a teacher, would you find this approach interesting and beneficial?

3. Provide several examples of nonlinguistic "ways of knowing."

4. Can you identify an assumption of schooling that merits further examination?

5. If you were to begin a charter school, what principles might you apply based on Eisner's critique of current practices?

Reading 9.2

Teaching Against Idiocy

Walter C. Parker
Phi Delta Kappan, January 2005

Can a democratic nation maintain its democracy if citizens pursue their own interests, sometimes at the expense of the greater good? And what does that have to do with schools, teachers, and "idiocy"? The author examines the term *idiocy* in its original form, a very different meaning from today's usage. The Greeks originally coined *idiocy* to mean selfish, self-centered, concerned with personal issues at the expense of the general good. The author argues that in order to maintain our liberties and freedoms as citizens in a democratic society, we must be more concerned about the greater good and in preserving our "democracy" (and less idiotic). The author believes it is the school's responsibility to give students the tools to become public-minded citizens. Educators can best accomplish this by modeling three actions: creating opportunities for interaction among students who are different from one another; planning deliberations around academic issues or common social problems; and defining the guidelines and parameters for effective deliberations. The author suggests that many history topics provide fruitful content for deliberation as well as common social problems.

Analysis Questions

1. Describe how the practices of so many Americans support the idiocy criticisms of the author.
2. Explain why the author believes it is important to educate children in the skill of effective deliberations.
3. Consider an example of a common social problem that you have encountered or possibly may encounter as a teacher. Prepare a mini-plan for a student deliberation around this issue.
4. The author is concerned with raising social consciousness and believes that schools are one way to do that. Do you agree with this idea? Explain.
5. Can nations also suffer from national selfishness? Explain.

Reading 9.3

Common Arguments About the Strengths and Limitations of Home Schooling

Michael H. Romanowski
The Clearing House, November/December 2001

In recent decades, home schooling in the United States has surged from approximately 15,000 students in 1984 to estimates that range between one and two million students. Michael Romanowski offers some arguments for and against home schooling. Advocates claim that home-schooled students develop closer relationships with their families and parents, have superior social skills and family values, benefit from attention and resources focused on only a fewer students, and are not influenced by negative social interactions found in traditional schools. Critics argue that home-schooled students are isolated and miss an integral part of the socialization process by not interacting with their peers on a regular basis. Critics also claim that individual families often do not have the funds to provide the same resources for teaching and that parents may not be qualified to teach, especially at the secondary level. A growing number of families are choosing to home-school their children, indicating a growing discontent with traditional school institutions.

Analysis Questions

1. Provide several arguments supporting the belief that home-schooled students are more socially adaptable than students attending traditional school institutions.

2. List the major criticisms and strengths of home schooling. Where do you stand on this issue?

3. The number of students being home-schooled has grown dramatically over the last two decades. To what do you attribute this increase?

4. Will the trend of increasing home-schooled students continue? Why or why not?

5. Should home-school parents be required to pass some minimum level of education or teacher preparation? Support your position.

Case Study 9.1

Allison Cohen: A teacher opens a resource room at a school that has never had any special education classrooms and believes the teachers are colluding to make the mainstreaming program fail.

Analysis Questions

1. Why are the Bidwell School teachers giving Allison so much trouble?

2. What are the problems here?
3. What can Allison do?

Case Study 9.2

Amy Rothman: A high school resource room teacher is confronted by a parent during a staffing meeting about a gifted, autistic student in her resource room for whom the parent wants a service not provided by the school district.

Analysis Questions

1. What are the major arguments for why Nathan should attend the college course?
2. What are the major arguments against Nathan attending this course?

3. If you were in the position to decide this case, what would you do?

Curriculum, Standards, and Testing

Readings

Case Studies

Reading 10.1

Welcome to Standardsville

Alan C. Jones
Phi Delta Kappan, February 2001

Alan Jones, a secondary school principal, provides a set of compelling, practitioner-based reasons why educational standards are not working to reform education in the United States. In his bleak black-and-white imaginary community of *Standardsville* (based on the film *Pleasantville*), conformity is celebrated, and teachers who bring color to their classrooms are terminated. The author argues that educational standards will not work because the United States is not black and white. Educational reform needs to be theory-based and student-centered, include the voices of educators, and bring more color to the educational landscape.

Analysis Questions

1. Do you agree with the author that teachers already have standards in the form of textbooks? Support your answer.
2. Discuss several ways in which education standards create burdens for teachers and school administrators.
3. Discuss the struggles that teachers face when implementing state learning standards in diverse classrooms. What effects do these standards have on bilingual students?
4. Can teachers implement standards while preserving their innovation in the classroom? How?
5. How do you think you will handle standards that you don't agree with?

Reading 10.2

No Child Left Behind: The Politics of Teacher Quality

Leslie Kaplan and William Ownings
Phi Delta Kappan, May 2003

Are certified teachers more effective in the classroom than uncertified teachers? Are teachers who have completed a teacher preparation program better qualified than content area experts? How has the No Child Left Behind law defined a "highly qualified" teacher? How do you? These controversial issues are at the heart of this article. Although there is consensus among educators and politicians that effective teachers positively affect student achievement, the evidence is more difficult to capture. One cannot generalize that all traditional teacher preparation programs or all alternative programs are effective. What preparation should you receive in order to become a successful teacher?

Analysis Questions

1. In what ways does the definition of *highly qualified* under No Child Left Behind fit or conflict with your view of what constitutes a high-quality teacher?

2. Do you feel that the requirement under NCLB for principals and master teachers to provide on-the-job training new teachers who are content experts is a reasonable one? How do you compare this training with a traditional teacher preparation program?

3. Explain several reasons why teacher quality research must be used and interpreted with caution.

4. Generally, what does the research suggest about the link between teacher preparation programs and teacher effectiveness?

5. How will this article influence your view and approach to teacher education?

Reading 10.3

How and Why Standards Can Improve Student Achievement: A Conversation with Robert J. Maranzo

Marge Scherer
Educational Leadership, September 2001

Although educational standards have yet to be effectively implemented, Mr. Maranzo makes the argument that standards hold the greatest hope for significantly improving student achievement in the United States. Although the current number and content of federal and state standards would require an extension of schooling to K-22 in order for them to be implemented completely, the standards movement has started an important conversation about what essential knowledge and skills should be addressed at each grade level. This step is an important one, but much still needs to be done to improve standards. Reducing the number of standards and cutting down the content within them will allow teachers more time to explore additional content of their choosing. Other changes that must be made before standards can be implemented effectively include closer and more frequent monitoring of student progress on the standards, and the adoption of a standards-based grading system.

Analysis Questions

1. Do you agree with the author's assertion that the standards movement has had more positive effects than negative on teachers and students? Support your answer.
2. Discuss several ways mentioned in the article in which standards can be improved.
3. Do you feel that standards-based education can coexist with instructional creativity? Defend your answer.
4. Discuss the distinction between "targets of knowledge and skills" and the "mandated level of knowledge and skills" that all students should achieve. Should the mandated achievement levels be a local, state, or national responsibility?
5. Are one-size-fits-all education standards appropriate for bilingual or for all groups of students? Explain your position.

Reading 10.4

Heightening Awareness About the Importance of Using Multicultural Literature

Susan A. Colby and Anna F. Lyon
Multicultural Education, Spring 2004

While America's schools have become increasingly diverse in recent years, this article suggests that prospective teacher awareness and understanding of multicultural issues have not kept pace. The authors analyzed the responses of 100 preservice teachers to a multicultural article entitled "African American Children's Literature That Helps Children Find Themselves: Selections for Grades K–3" (Hefflin and Barksdale-Ladd, 2001). Many of the prospective teachers had not previously considered how the predominately white curriculum affects African American students and other underrepresented students. Being able to "see" yourself in the curriculum is important. The new information the prospective teachers gained through this activity offered important insights into the benefits of incorporating multicultural literature into classroom activities.

Analysis Questions

1. Why do you think that so many of the prospective teachers were unaware of the lack of African-American literature in many schools of the past and present?
2. Do you believe that only African American students benefit from incorporating African American literature into the classroom?
3. Provide several examples of the benefits of multicultural literature for *all* students. What are some of the social issues that using multicultural literature can create space for in the classroom?
4. What is the effect of the "colorblind lens" through which many white teachers and students see people?
5. What are some practical ways that well-intentioned teachers can overcome the "unintentional discrimination" that may be present in their classrooms?

Reading 10.5

Where Did We Come From?

Lottie L. Joiner
American School Board Journal, April 2003

If you thought the controversy over teaching about the theory of evolution was over, this article will bring you up to date. Joiner illustrates the challenges that many state boards of education face today in developing science curriculum standards for the topic of evolution. Whereas the teaching of *creationism* (the approach that employs religious beliefs to explain the origin of the species) has been ruled a violation of the principle of separation of church and state, a new theory about the origin of species, called *intelligent design*, is the source of much controversy. Intelligent design asserts that chance alone cannot explain the creation of the universe, and that science to date has been unable to. Therefore, there is intentionality, an intelligent design behind creation. In Ohio, for example, new science curriculum standards have expanded the teaching of evolution to include not only Charles Darwin's theory, but also an analysis and discussion of scientific criticisms of evolution, of how that theory falls short.

Analysis Questions

1. In what ways have court decisions changed what is taught in American public schools about evolution?
2. Do you believe that the theory of intelligent design should be included in public science education? Why or why not?
3. Why does the science educator Eugene Scott consider the inclusion of intelligent design in the curriculum to be "irresponsible"?
4. Should community morals and values influence what is included in the curriculum for the topic of evolution? Defend your answer.
5. Should fear of an explanation beyond science exclude hypotheses that cannot be proven? Can intelligent design exist beyond the bounds of current religious beliefs?

Reading 10.6

Closing the Gender Gap—Again!

David Sadker and Karen Zittleman
Principal, March/April 2005

If you thought that gender bias was an issue of the past, this article suggests that you take another look. The authors provide examples of how gender influences today's course enrollments and the career choices made by girls and boys, as well as insights into how current school practices serve to reinforce gender differences and stereotyping. Part of the challenge confronting educators is to understand that gender stereotyping is not a "female issue," but one that curtails the options of both boys and girls. Boys do not grow up in isolation from social forces, and they too feel the pressure of gender expectations. The challenge of actually "seeing" how gender shapes schools has been made more difficult by No Child Left Behind, which, while requiring test scores of many demographic groups, does not ask schools to analyze gender differences in scoring.

Analysis Questions

1. Why do you believe that gender stereotyping has been such an intractable educational issue?

2. Offer several examples of how gender bias affects the lives of students and teachers.

3. Can you offer arguments for and against creating single-sex schools? (Make certain to include the impact of such schools on both males and females in your response.)

4. How might you track/monitor your own classroom behavior to ensure that gender bias is not an unintentional part of your teaching, of your "hidden curriculum"?

5. Suggest several affirmative steps you can take to help both boys and girls overcome the limiting restrictions of gender stereotyping.

Reading 10.7

Gender Bias in Teacher Education Texts: New (and Old) Lessons

Karen Zittleman and David Sadker
Journal of Teacher Education, March/April 2002

If you expect teacher education textbooks to contain substantial amounts of information about gender issues in education, you're in for a rude awakening. Although gender-related teaching ideas can easily be found in the news media and popular books, Zittleman and Sadker's content analysis of the leading teacher education texts reveals that gender and gender bias issues are given minimal, if any, coverage. Few of the texts contain discussions of specific strategies to confront gender stereotypes and promote gender fairness. How to help boys overcome their reading problems, or help girls confront barriers in science or math, is the kind of topic teachers learn little, if anything, about. The texts that do cover gender issues often do so in the form of boxed-off inserts, which reinforces the peripheral treatment of these important issues. The authors suggest that until teacher education texts are altered to give adequate attention to gender issues, the elimination of gender bias will rely on the creativity of teachers.

Analysis Questions

1. What are some possible explanations for the exclusion of important gender bias issues in teacher education textbooks?
2. What were you most surprised about in reading the section on Title IX?
3. Given the current public debate on the gender gap that exists in math and science courses, how can you explain the minimal coverage of gender issues in math and science teaching methods textbooks?
4. Where might you go to uncover strategies to help boys overcome their reading difficulties?
5. Brainstorm some of the subtle practices and things that you should be aware of in your classroom in order to create a more equitable classroom environment for both males and females.

Case Study 10.1

Elaine Adams: A student teacher near the end of her assignment observes her cooperating teacher give the students help while administering the district-mandated standardized tests. She finds herself unsure how to deal with the situation.

Analysis Questions

1. Did Ms. Green go too far in helping her students?

2. If you challenged her, how would Ms. Green answer the above question?

3. What should Elaine Adams do?

Case Study 10.2

Jim Colbert: A third-grade teacher in an inner-city school is trying his best to teach language arts using basal readers and a district-required curriculum. He is especially concerned about one Spanish-speaking child who appears to want to learn but who speaks English only at school.

Analysis Questions

1. What are Jim Colbert's strengths and weaknesses as a teacher?

2. What are Carlos' strengths and weaknesses as a learner?

3. What would you identify as the most important problems in this situation?

Case Study 10.3

Melinda Grant: A teacher who has developed an innovative curriculum is concerned because another teacher continually warns her that she will be held responsible for her students' end-of-year standardized test scores.

Analysis Questions

1. How does Melinda see her problem? Do you agree with her?

2. What is the role of standardized tests in schools? Do they provide teachers with information? With direction? Should they?

3. What do you think Melinda should do?

Chapter 11

Becoming an Effective Teacher

Readings

Case Studies

Reading 11.1

Good Teachers, Plural

Donald R. Cruickshank and Donald Haefele
Educational Leadership, February 2001

Although our current vision of "good teachers" relies heavily upon how well their students perform on standardized tests, this has not always been the case. Throughout the 20th century, our vision of good teachers has varied from relying on subjective standards to the current emphasis on standardized test scores. In this article, the authors discuss several different visions of good teachers, and conclude that no one type is superior to all others. The authors argue that we need to expand our vision of "good teachers" to include multiple types, and that we must also create systems of teacher evaluation that correspond to each of the recognized models.

Analysis Questions

1. What patterns do you notice in the visions of good teachers over time? What forces do you think drive these changes?
2. What role does student achievement testing have on the vision of good teachers?
3. Discuss the distinction between expert teachers and experienced teachers.

How do you think one goes about developing expertise as a teacher?

4. Which vision(s) of good teachers gets at the heart of what you think it means to be a good teacher? How does this vision(s) relate to your preferred philosophy(ies) of education?

Reading 11.2

The Engaged Classroom

Sam M. Intrator
Educational Leadership, September 2004

Although students generally describe their time in high schools as boring and monotonous, classrooms can also be dynamic and engaging places where dreams are created and nurtured. In this article, we get a look at the fascinating school research of Sam Intrator, who spent 130 days shadowing students in one California high school. The goal of this research was to determine what is going on in the classroom experiences and in students' hearts when they are completely engaged. In this article, we are taken on a tour of both disengaged classroom episodes and engaged episodes. Several examples of "anti-boredom pedagogy" reveal that engaging teachers give students the chance to express their originality and be creative. Engaging teachers know their students on a personal level and are able to create important bridges between the subject being learned and the personal experiences of their students. By winning their students' hearts and minds, teachers can create opportunities for students to find value and meaning in their educational experiences.

Analysis Questions

1. Reflect back on your experiences in middle and/or high school. Would you characterize the majority of the time you spent in school as engaged or disengaged? What characterized the classroom environments and teachers that stand out to you as being the most engaging?

2. Think of some ways in which teachers can bring energy and creativity into the classroom.

3. What are some commonalities of the disengaged times described in the article? What lessons do these episodes provide for you as a teacher or future teacher?

4. What lessons have you gained about engaging students, and how can you translate this information into the classroom?

Reading 11.3

Personalized Instruction

James W. Keefe and John M. Jenkins
Phi Delta Kappan, February 2002

Amid the negative connotations of today's school reform efforts, James Keefe and John Jenkins promote a focus on a different kind of reform, school "renewal" through *personalized instruction*. Personalized instruction at its heart involves the creation of learning settings that value individual student characteristics and needs, and the use of flexible instruction practices. The six basic elements of personalized instruction are (1) the dual teacher role as a teacher-coach and teacher-advisor, (2) diagnosis of student learning characteristics, (3) the school culture of collegiality and collaboration, (4) interactive learning environments, (5) flexible scheduling and pacing, and (6) authentic assessment. The curriculum of a school using personalized instruction is centered on the developmental needs of its students, and hands-on collaborative activities are emphasized.

Analysis Questions

1. Discuss the distinction between school "reform" and school "renewal." How does personalized instruction fit into the process of school "renewal"?

2. Discuss the dual teacher role in personalized instruction. How do these roles differ from more teacher-centered education approaches?

3. How does personalized instruction's focus on the assessment of developmental characteristics of students conflict with our current standards and high-stakes testing movement?

4. How could you translate the information discussed about the culture of collegiality into specific classroom norms and practices?

5. Discuss the pros and cons of both authentic assessments and standardized tests. Consider the viewpoints of both teachers and students.

Reading 11.4

Where's the Content? The Role of Content in Constructivist Teacher Education

Sam Hausfather
Educational Horizons, Fall 2001

Although constructivism is a popular education approach, its meaning is frequently misunderstood by both teachers and the public. Constructivist theory contends that knowledge is actively constructed through human interaction with one another and with the physical world, and that knowledge is based upon student experiences and prior knowledge. Constructivist teaching erases the division between content and the process of learning by linking the knowledge of content with the use of content. The author suggests that teacher education programs model themselves after the constructivist approach by having teacher education faculty collaborate with arts and science faculty in order to create courses that integrate strong disciplinary content preparation with preparation in teaching methodology and pedagogy. Also discussed are ways to incorporate the role of prior knowledge, and the social nature of knowledge into constructivist teacher education programs.

Analysis Questions

1. Why do you think that constructivism is so frequently misunderstood? What are some likely causes of criticism?
2. Discuss the link between the content and process of learning in an ideal constructivist teacher education program.
3. Brainstorm ideas of how to incorporate multiple forms of knowledge, the role of prior knowledge, and the social nature of knowledge into a constructivist teacher education program.
4. What is the goal of "pedagogical content knowledge"? How can teacher education programs help achieve this goal?
5. Describe what a constructivist-based classroom looks like. What teaching methods are used? Do you foresee any challenges with implementing this approach today?

Reading 11.5

The Web's Impact on Student Learning

Katrina A. Meyer
T.H.E. Journal Online, May 2003

In this article, Katrina Meyer presents findings from her review of current research studies of college distance learning practices. Although there is still much to learn in the field of distance learning education research, this article provides three general themes: individual differences, instructional design, and improved skills. In order to maximize the effectiveness of distance learning, instructional methods should be matched with student learning styles. Research suggests that the success of distance learning courses has much to do with the instructional design of the course rather than solely the technology, but the separate effects of technology and instruction have yet to be determined. Online learning courses can also support the development of critical thinking and writing skills. Much remains to be uncovered in the field of Web-based learning. Ms. Meyer contends that rather than asking generally whether the Web affects learning, future research must explore the educational effectiveness of specific technologies for specific types of students, specific subjects, and specific purposes.

Analysis Questions

1. Discuss the methodological problem with research that compares Web-based courses to traditional courses.
2. What are the different experiences of males and females in online learning courses? Do you think that online learning enhances or reduces the presence of gender bias in education?
3. How can instructional design be effectively used to encourage interaction among students and between the teacher and students?
4. Do you think that e-communities are a valuable component of distance learning? Explain your answer.
5. How could you apply the lessons learned from this article to the K–12 education setting?

Reading 11.6

The Winding Path: Understanding the Career Cycle of Teachers

Susan K. Lynn
The Clearing House, March/April 2002

This article provides an interesting view of the phases teachers pass through in their own career cycle, and how this cycle relates to teacher development theory. The author describes how professional development opportunities should be personalized to the individual needs of teachers during each career phase. Teacher development theory also suggests that a teacher's personal environment and organizational environment will affect his/her position within the career cycle. As a result, Ms. Lynn suggests that greater attention must be paid to the personal needs and problems of teachers. Not surprisingly, supportive and nurturing organizational environments can support teachers at all stages and create positive career progression.

Analysis Questions

1. Can you think of any other environments in addition to personal and organizational that could affect a teacher's career cycle?
2. Brainstorm some actions that school administrators can take in order to create and maintain supportive and nurturing environments for teachers.
3. How do you think awareness of the teacher career cycle can help you if you find yourself in a negative career progression?
4. Why might some teachers be hesitant to seek or accept support for their personal needs or problems?

Ken Kelly: A teacher having trouble with questioning and with discussion teaching visits a teacher who is holding a Socratic discussion with a fourth-grade class. He questions the applicability of her methods to his situation.

Analysis Questions

1. Why was Ken's lesson unsuccessful?
2. Why did Sybil Avilla's lesson work?
3. Can Ken use Sybil's techniques in his class? Why/why not and how?

Case Study 11.2

Judith Kent: A teacher engages her students in whole-class discussion, and then the students work with partners on an assignment. She explains the planning process she went through to reteach the lesson after it had not worked in the previous class.

Analysis Questions

1. How would you describe Judith Kent's teaching style? Her philosophy of education?
2. Try to analyze her instructional practices from the perspective of the principles of instruction. What is she doing well? What areas would you want her to improve?
3. Would you want to be in Judith's class if you were a fifth-grade student? Why/why not?

Case Study 11.3

Melissa Reid: An enthusiastic young student teacher struggles to gain the respect and improve the behavior of her senior-level composition class and is devastated by one of her student's papers, which is full of vindictiveness and hatred toward her.

Analysis Questions

1. Melissa Reid's student teaching experience goes from good to bad very quickly here. To what do you attribute this?
2. Is Melissa following good classroom management practice?
3. What should she do about James' threat?

Topic Index

	Accountability and Standards	Assessment and High-Stakes Testing	Bilingual Education	Bullying	Character Education and Values	Classroom Climate and Management	Community	Constructivism	Curriculum	Democratic Education	Diversity, Multicultural	
Reading 1.1 **Keeping Good Teachers: Why It Matters, What Leaders Can Do,** Linda Darling Hammond		X										
Reading 1.2 **How to Build a Better Teacher,** Robert Holland												
Reading 1.3 **Metaphors of Hope,** Mimi Brodsky Chenfeld						X			X	X		
Reading 2.1 Text excerpt from *Race Matters,* Cornel West							X			X	X	
Reading 2.2 **Language Learning: A Worldwide Perspective,** Donna Christian, Ingrid U. Pufahl, and Nancy C. Rhodes			X						X			
Reading 2.3 **Profoundly Multicultural Questions,** Sonia M. Nieto			X						X		X	
Reading 2.4 **Discipline and the Special Education Student,** James A. Taylor and Richard A. Baker, Jr.						X						
Reading 3.1 **Bullying Among Children,** Janis R. Bullock				X		X						
Reading 3.2 **Differentiating Sexualities in Singular Classrooms,** Kevin J. Graziano						X					X	
Reading 3.3 **Meeting the Challenge of the Urban High School,** Joyce Baldwin							X					
Reading 3.4 **Creating School Climates That Prevent School Violence,** Reece L. Peterson and Russell Skiba				X	X	X	X					
Reading 3.5 **Profiles in Caring: Teachers Who Create Learning Communities in Their Classrooms,** David Strahan, et al.						X	X				X	
Reading 4.1 Text excerpt from *The Education of Free Men,* Horace Mann										X	X	
Reading 4.2 **The Changing Landscape of U.S. Education,** James C. Carper												
Reading 4.3 **Dichotomizing Education: Why No One Wins and America Loses,** Carl D. Glickman												
Reading 4.4 Text excerpts from *Eighty Years and More (1815–1897): Reminiscences of Elizabeth Cady Stanton,* Elizabeth Cady Stanton												

	Education Law	Ethics	Gender	History of Education	Home Schooling	Induction/Mentoring	Instruction	No Child Left Behind	Parents	Philosophy of Education	Reform	Religion	School Culture and Climate	School Finance and Governance	Schools	Social Justice	Student Learning, Motivation and	Students	Students with Special Needs	Teacher Effectiveness	Teacher Education and Licensure	Teachers	Technology	Urban Education
						X		X		X				X						X	X	X		
						X	X			X							X			X	X	X		
																		X				X		
																X								X
							X														X		X	
	X													X		X	X	X				X		
	X																		X					
										X						X		X				X		
			X				X					X				X		X				X		
				X							X		X		X		X	X				X		X
							X						X		X			X				X		X
																		X				X		X
				X											X									
	X		X								X	X			X									
			X							X	X				X									
			X	X								X											X	

	Accountability and Standards	Assessment and High-Stakes Testing	Bilingual Education	Bullying	Character Education and Values	Classroom Climate and Management	Community	Constructivism	Curriculum	Democratic Education	Diversity, Multicultural	
Reading 5.1 **The Threat of Stereotype**, Joshua Aronson		X									X	
Reading 5.2 Text excerpts from ***Narrative of the Life of Frederick Douglass: An American Slave,*** Frederick Douglass											X	
Reading 5.3 **An Educator's Primer to the Gender War**, David Sadker		X									X	
Reading 6.1 Text excerpts from ***Experience and Education,*** John Dewey									X			
Reading 6.2 **Pathways to Reform: Start with Values**, David Ferrero, Jr.							X		X		X	
Reading 6.3 **Teaching Themes of Care**, Nel Noddings									X			
Reading 6.4 **A Tale of Two Schools**, Larry Cuban										X		
Reading 7.1 Text excerpt from ***Amazing Grace,*** Jonathan Kozol							X				X	
Reading 7.2 **The Culture Builder**, Roland S. Barth												
Reading 7.3 **The Invisible Role of the Central Office**, Kathleen F. Grove	X											
Reading 8.1 **How Not to Teach Values: A Critical Look at Character Education**, Alfie Kohn					X	X	X	X	X			
Reading 8.2 **Teaching About Religion**, Susan Black									X		X	
Reading 8.3 **Decisions That Have Shaped U.S. Education**, Perry Zirkel			X			X					X	
Reading 8.4 **Andy's Right to Privacy in Grading and the *Falvo* v. *Owasso Public Schools* Case**, Stephan J. Friedman		X										
Reading 9.1 **Questionable Assumptions About Schooling**, Elliot W. Eisner		X							X			
Reading 9.2 **Teaching Against Idiocy**, Walter C. Parker									X	X	X	
Reading 9.3 **Common Arguments About the Strengths and Limitations of Home Schooling**, Michael H. Romanowski					X				X		X	
Reading 10.1 **Welcome to Standardsville**, Alan C. Jones	X											
Reading 10.2 **No Child Left Behind: The Politics of Teacher Quality**, Leslie Kaplan and William Ownings												
Reading 10.3 **How and Why Standards Can Improve Student Achievement: A Conversation with Robert J. Maranzo**, Marge Scherer	X	X							X			

	Accountability and Standards	Assessment and High-Stakes Testing	Bilingual Education	Bullying	Character Education and Values	Classroom Climate and Management	Community	Constructivism	Curriculum	Democratic Education	Diversity, Multicultural	
Reading 10.4 **Heightening Awareness About the Importance of Using Multicultural Literature,** Susan A. Colby and Anna F. Lyon									X		X	
Reading 10.5 **Where Did We Come From?**, Lottie L. Joiner	X								X			
Reading 10.6 **Closing the Gender Gap—Again!**, David Sadker and Karen Zittleman		X		X							X	
Reading 10.7 **Gender Bias in Teacher Education Texts: New (and Old) Lessons**, Karen Zittleman and David Sadker											X	
Reading 11.1 **Good Teachers, Plural**, Donald R. Cruickshank and Donald Haefele												
Reading 11.2 **The Engaged Classroom**, Sam M. Intrator						X						
Reading 11.3 **Personalized Instruction**, James W. Keefe and John M. Jenkins		X				X		X			X	
Reading 11.4 **Where's the Content? The Role of Content in Constructivist Teacher Education**, Sam Hausfather								X				
Reading 11.5 **The Web's Impact on Student Learning,** Katrina A. Meyer												
Reading 11.6 **The Winding Path: Understanding the Career Cycle of Teachers,** Susan K. Lynn												
Case Study 1.1 Megan Brownlee		X				X						
Case Study 1.2 Jennifer Gordon						X					X	
Case Study 2.1 Carol Brown						X					X	
Case Study 2.2 Carolyn Davis		X				X						
Case Study 2.3 Joan Martin, Marilyn Coe, & Warren Groves						X		X				
Case Study 3.1 Bonnie Bradley						X						
Case Study 3.2 Richard Carlton						X						
Case Study 3.3 Anne Holt						X						
Case Study 5.1 Helen Franklin									X		X	
Case Study 5.2 Leigh Scott		X									X	
Case Study 5.3 Mark Siegal											X	
Case Study 6.1 Brenda Forester												
Case Study 6.2 Michael Watson						X						

	Education Law	Ethics	Gender	History of Education	Home Schooling	Induction/Mentoring	Instruction	No Child Left Behind	Parents	Philosophy of Education	Reform	Religion	School Culture and Climate	School Finance and Governance	Schools	Social Justice	Student Learning, Motivation and	Students	Students with Special Needs	Teacher Effectiveness	Teacher Education and Licensure	Teachers	Technology	Urban Education
																		X			X	X		
												X												
			X				X	X														X	X	
	X		X				X								X						X			
	X			X						X										X	X	X		
							X												X	X		X		
							X				X		X				X		X		X	X		
							X										X			X	X			
			X				X										X						X	
						X															X		X	
																				X	X		X	
																				X	X			
																				X				
																				X				
						X														X				
							X											X						
							X													X	X			
							X													X	X	X		
						X	X																	
																				X				
						X	X										X			X				
						X	X			X												X		
							X			X												X		

	Accountability and Standards	Assessment and High-Stakes Testing	Bilingual Education	Bullying	Character Education and Values	Classroom Climate and Management	Community	Constructivism	Curriculum	Democratic Education	Diversity, Multicultural	
Case Study 7.1 David Burton						X					X	
Case Study 7.2 Kate Sullivan			X								X	
Case Study 7.3 Jane Vincent		X				X						
Case Study 8.1 Amanda Jackson												
Case Study 8.2 Ellen Norton												
Case Study 8.3 Diane News		X									X	
Case Study 9.1 Allison Cohen						X						
Case Study 9.2 Amy Rothman												
Case Study 10.1 Elaine Adams			X									
Case Study 10.2 Jim Colbert		X				X						
Case Study 10.3 Melinda Grant		X							X			
Case Study 11.1 Ken Kelly						X			X			
Case Study 11.2 Judith Kent						X					X	
Case Study 11.3 Melissa Reid												

Education Law	Ethics	Gender	History of Education	Home Schooling	Induction/Mentoring	Instruction	No Child Left Behind	Parents	Philosophy of Education	Reform	Religion	School Culture and Climate	School Finance and Governance	Schools	Social Justice	Student Learning, Motivation and	Students	Students with Special Needs	Teacher Effectiveness	Teacher Education and Licensure	Teachers	Technology	Urban Education
	X																			X		X	
								X												X	X		X
																X	X						
	X				X																		
	X																X						
		X					X																
												X						X					
X								X										X					
																				X			
					X	X							X										X
									X														
						X			X								X						
						X												X					
																				X			